James Through the Eyes of Paul

JAMES
Through the Eyes of Paul

DONNA HUGHEY

RESOURCE *Publications* · Eugene, Oregon

JAMES THROUGH THE EYES OF PAUL

Resource Publications
An Imprint of Wipf and Stock Publishers
199 W. 8th Ave., Suite 3
Eugene, OR 97401

www.wipfandstock.com

ISBN 13: 978-1-4982-0176-6

Manufactured in the U.S.A.   09/22/2014

Contents

Introduction

The book of James offers practical advice about dealing with people, the church, society, and even ourselves. As a result, many believers consider the book to be a "how-to guide" for being a Christian. But James's letter doesn't only deliver practical advice; it also critically examines a believer's relationship with God. James delivers a deep message about the role faith plays in everything we do.

In the early Christian church, however, James's letter was sometimes thought to be in conflict with the writings of Paul. While Paul's letters strongly emphasize salvation solely through faith, James's letter places great emphasis on good works. At first glance, this does seem to be a contradiction—so much so that early church leaders nearly excluded the book of James from scripture.

In this Bible study, we'll work through the book of James, using Paul's letters to add more depth and greater context to James's message. We'll see that not only do James and Paul agree, but together they offer incredible insights about our relationship with God. James and Paul, through their letters, will provide us with a complementary discussion of faith, obedience, and our responsibilities to God. We'll also develop a deeper understanding of vital biblical truths: we'll learn what we believe, how to apply those beliefs to our lives, and why our faith is so important. Together, this will help us better understand the purpose of our faith and what's expected of us as followers of God.

Maybe that makes James a great how-to guide, after all.

1

The Testing of Faith

James 1:1–12

✤ SUMMARY

James's goal is to teach believers the perspective, attitude, and behavior necessary to guide and sustain their Christian faith throughout their lives. But to do this, James must first teach his readers to change the way they look at things—to change their perspective—because if they don't, they'll never be able to change their attitudes. And a right attitude is key to changing and correcting bad behavior.

He begins by telling us that instead of feeling sorry for ourselves when we're facing trials, we should rejoice. After all, trials produce perseverance, and perseverance produces a more mature faith. While our instinct may be to grumble and complain when things aren't going our way, James tells us that only through hardship can we truly develop our faith and maturity as believers. That's a reason to rejoice: hardship makes us better believers. And it's that perspective that James wants us to adopt.

James goes on to say that every believer will face tests, trials, and hardships, regardless of station, because all believers need to further develop their faith. Those who endure and persevere through hardships—by leaning and depending on the wisdom of God—will be richly rewarded.

✺ GETTING THE BASICS

READ JAMES 1:1–4.

1. What kind of attitude does James tell us to have when we face a hard situation?

2. What does the testing of faith produce?

3. What benefit do believers gain by persevering through trials?

4. If we know that trials develop perseverance, which in turn helps us mature as Christians, what are we saying about God if we have bad attitudes during hardships?

READ ACTS 16:19–40.

5. These verses provide a great example of how Paul and Silas persevered while undergoing extreme circumstances. Why do you think Paul and Silas were able to rejoice during this situation?

James teaches believers to rejoice when undergoing hardships and Paul does just that—praying and singing hymns while imprisoned in Philippi. While scripture does not record Paul's prayer, his actions speak volumes about his faith, Christian maturity, and trust in God. In a way, this illustrates the relationship between the teachings of James and Paul: have faith, and then be guided by that faith in your actions.

6. The actions of Paul and Silas while in prison affected those around them. What does this teach us about the effect our attitudes can have on others when we're facing trials?

❧ DIGGING DEEPER

READ JAMES 1:5–8.

7. James tells us to ask God for wisdom. How can godly wisdom help us during trials and hardships?

8. How does James describe a person who asks God for wisdom but then doubts?

READ JAMES 1:9–11.

9. James says a person "in humble circumstances ought to take pride in his high position." What do you think this means, and how does this display godly wisdom?

READ PHILIPPIANS 4:11–13.

10. How does Paul display his Christian maturity and wisdom?

James and Paul are in complete agreement regarding Christian maturity and wisdom. Only through faith and perseverance can believers grow and flourish as followers of Christ, and both men stress this in their letters. But Christian maturity doesn't happen overnight. Paul tells us that he has "learned the secret" (Philippians 4:12)—indicating that it took time for his Christian maturity to develop. It was through his many trials and hardships that Paul learned to trust and depend on God; through this perseverance, Paul grew in faith and maturity. Just as James hopes for us, Paul lacked for nothing as a result (James 1:4).

READ JAMES 1:12.

11. What promise does God make to those who endure trials?

READ 1 CORINTHIANS 9:24–25.

12. How does Paul describe God's reward for enduring a lifetime of trials?

READ ROMANS 8:18.

13. Why does Paul believe that, ultimately, our suffering is not important?

Both James and Paul place the right level of importance on trials. Yes, they happen, but they are neither the point of Christianity nor the end result. Trials come and go, but what remains is the glory of our everlasting salvation. Therefore, believers should use trials as tools to build perseverance, patience, and a stronger foundation for their faith.

❀ SOMETHING TO THINK ABOUT: SUFFERING

Like Paul, many godly men and women endured unspeakable circumstances throughout scripture. The same is true today. We find sickness, sorrow, and suffering everywhere we look. But suffering has not always existed. In the beginning, man lived in complete harmony with God, and it was only after man chose to sin that suffering entered the world (Genesis 3).

People who blame God for their suffering fail to realize that hardships are a consequence of this original sin, not of an unjust God. Paul is emphatic about this, telling us we suffer because we are sinners and fall short of the glory of God (Romans 3:23). While pain and suffering are never easy, both James and Paul teach that once we set our minds on God and stop focusing on our hardship, our faith will grow stronger and deeper, producing endurance and maturity.

2

Temptation

James 1:13–18

❈ SUMMARY

James began his letter by describing how believers will benefit by persevering through trials. He told us that perseverance helps us develop a stronger, deeper faith and maturity. Here, James makes sure we understand that trials are not the same thing as temptation, which is born out of our own evil desires. God rewards perseverance, but James does not want believers to think that God tempts them as part of a trial. Instead, temptation is something else altogether, and God has no role in it.

James makes it very clear that God does not tempt anyone and that believers are responsible for their own sin. He explains that sin is tied to our ungodly desires, and when we sin, it separates us from God. He concludes by describing God's unfailing goodness—a goodness that's a direct contrast from the sinful desires of our own hearts.

✸ GETTING THE BASICS

READ JAMES 1:13–15.

1. What does James say is the cause of temptation?

2. What are the three stages of temptation?

READ 1 CORINTHIANS 7:5 AND 1 THESSALONIANS 3:5.

3. According to these verses, who is the tempter?

Temptation originates from two sources: from our own sinful desires and from Satan. Although scripture teaches that all *evil* originates with Satan, our sinful nature can tempt us just as strongly as Satan himself. Despite the fact that all believers have the Holy Spirit residing in their hearts, we still possess a corrupt and fallen human nature, which is in direct conflict with our new self.

Even Paul struggled with this conflict and tells us in Romans 7:21–23, "So I find this law at work: When I want to do good, evil is right there with me. For in my inner being I delight in God's law; but I see another law at work in the members of my body, waging war against the law of my mind and making me a prisoner of sin at work within my members."

READ 1 CORINTHIANS 10:12 AND GALATIANS 6:1.

4. What warning does Paul give believers about temptation?

READ EPHESIANS 6:10–18.

5. Paul uses the imagery of a soldier's armor to teach believers how to prepare themselves against evil, which can also include sin and temptations. List each strength that God has made available to every believer.

READ 1 CORINTHIANS 10:13.

6. Paul offers us a powerful promise from God while being tempted. What is that promise?

There's a difference between being tempted and sinning. Temptation usually begins as an unrighteous thought and sin is the unrighteous action following that thought. Remember what James says: ". . . after desire has conceived, it gives birth to sin; and sin, when it is full-grown, gives birth to death." In other words, temptation—the sinful thoughts that grow out of our earthly desires—can lead to sinful action, which in turn separates us from God. By learning not to dwell on evil thoughts, and by focusing our thoughts on righteousness, we can resist the temptations that lead to sin.

❁ DIGGING DEEPER

READ JAMES 1:16–17.

7. What does James warn his readers about in verse 16?

READ 2 CORINTHIANS 13:5.

8. How can we make sure we aren't deceiving ourselves into thinking we are "in the faith" when in actuality, we may not be?

READ ROMANS 8:5–9.

9. What does how we live our lives say about our commitment to Christ?

Some people think they are true Christians as long as they publicly claim to follow Christ, regardless of how they live their lives. But that isn't true. In fact, it's the change in our thinking, and the outward actions that coincide with those thoughts, that prove a real and genuine transformation has occurred. Both James and Paul teach that it's possible for a person to deceive themselves into thinking they are a believer when they are not. To guard against this self-deception, Paul tells us to test and examine ourselves, which undoubtedly will reveal if our actions and behaviors align with what we say we believe.

10. Who does James say is the giver of every good and perfect gift?

11. Why do you think James needs to remind us that all good things come from God?

After discussing temptation, James switches back to the subject of trials. James knew that sometimes in the midst of hardship, people forget who God is, or even worse, start to believe that God has abandoned them. James didn't want this sort of thinking to take root, so he spends some time focusing on the goodness of God, reminding his readers that God chooses to bless them through every good and perfect gift they receive. James emphasizes that even during our worst trials, God is with us, provides us with every blessing, and will never turn away.

READ JAMES 1:18 AND 2 CORINTHIANS 5:17.

12. How do both James and Paul describe a person who has come to faith in God?

READ EPHESIANS 2:1–2.

13. Why does a person need to be born again?

14. What do you think it means that God considers us "a kind of first fruits of all he created?"

In the Old Testament, the first fruits were the best parts of a crop, which were then offered to God as an act of worship and praise for all that he had provided (Deuteronomy 26:1-10). With this background in mind, James draws from the Old Testament custom of first fruits and tells us that believers are the best of all that God has created.

❈ SOMETHING TO THINK ABOUT: TRIALS AND TEMPTATIONS

James told us to focus on God throughout trials (James 1:12), and Paul warned us to always remain alert for temptations (Galatians 6:1). While these are both great teachings, it's important for believers to understand the difference between the trials and temptations. By understanding the difference, believers are in better position to react to what they're facing.

Simply put, a trial is a set of circumstances—often ongoing, over a period of time—that can help a believer become stronger, more faithful, and more dependent on God, all without causing sin. In fact, with a trial, there is no obvious sin to commit. Financial hardship is a good example of a trial.

Temptation, on the other hand, is often fueled by sinful desires, and it can cause a believer to stumble and sin in a very clear way. Temptation generally comes down to a single act—if the action is taken, it ceases being a temptation and becomes sin. An example of temptation may be the desire to steal, or to commit adultery.

Now that we understand the difference between the two, how are we to react? The ideal response to a trial is, "I should depend on God and have faith," followed by prayer for strength, perseverance, and endurance. The ideal response to temptation is, "I should not do this," followed by prayer for strength and a commitment to godly behavior.

By understanding what we're actually being confronted with, we're in a better position to respond and behave in a way that's pleasing to God. Just by asking ourselves a simple question—"Am I being tempted to do something that will result with me sinning?"—we can identify our circumstances and respond accordingly, either by persevering through our trial or resisting the temptation.

Remember, a trial is meant to be persevered, while a temptation is meant to be overcome.

3

Listening and Acting on the Word of God

James 1:19–27

❁ SUMMARY

The basic teaching in this section is simple: be quick to listen, don't get angry, practice what you've learned, and watch what you say. But after taking a closer look, we'll realize that James's message is much deeper. Twice he warns believers not to deceive themselves into thinking they're religious and obedient if all they're doing is hearing God's truth. If a person is not being obedient, if they are not acting on what they've learned, then that person actually has a dead faith. It isn't enough to say we're followers of God and then go on living our lives however we choose—there has to be a change in our lives, evidence that the word of God has taken root in our hearts.

James understood the difference between *knowing* the truth and *living* the truth, and he touched on this subject back in earlier verses when he described a person who was "double-minded"—one who is confused in his thoughts and behavior. That type of person is trying to walk in two directions at the same time, which only causes doubt, inner conflict, and turmoil. Only by responding to God's word and putting his teachings in action can a believer trust that he is living as God intended.

❋ GETTING THE BASICS

READ JAMES 1:19–20.

1. What instruction does James offer his readers in these verses?

2. What kind of life does God desire for his followers?

READ JAMES 1:21.

3. What does James tell us to rid ourselves of?

READ ROMANS 1:28–31.

4.   What does Paul describe as immoral, evil, and worldly behavior?

People have a tendency to become ill-tempered when things aren't going their way, and this is especially true in times of difficulty and stress. But James teaches that the old attitudes we once had before becoming believers are to be replaced with the new attitudes we've learned through God's word. Paul gives us some examples of those old attitudes, and we can clearly see how they no longer have a place in the life of a believer. But more importantly, by practicing what we've learned, James says we'll live the righteous life that God desires for us.

READ EPHESIANS 4:22–24.

5.   How does Paul compare our "old self" with our "new self"?

REREAD JAMES 1:21.

6. James was writing to believers who had already accepted Christ. How do you think believers—who have already received salvation—might be "saved" by following his instruction?

It's only by having the correct attitudes and actions that we can live the kinds of lives God intends for us. By ridding ourselves of immoral behavior and replacing it with godly behavior, we gain the strength we need to overcome testing and trials. It ends up being quite circular: endure testing, which helps you live rightly, which helps you better endure testing, which helps you live rightly, and so on. In a way, that's the "saving" that James is talking about here. We already have salvation, but the truth can still save us from ourselves in our daily lives.

❀ DIGGING DEEPER

READ JAMES 1:22.

7. What does James say we do when we "merely listen to the word"?

8.   How can we avoid deceiving ourselves?

Deception runs throughout the Bible, beginning in Genesis 3:13 with the serpent deceiving Eve in Eden. But James isn't talking about the deception of others in these verses—he's talking about self-deception, a deception that causes a person to see the faults and sins of others while remaining blinded to his own.

READ JAMES 1:23–25.

9.   How should we receive God's word?

READ TITUS 1:16.

10. How does Paul compare belief in God to outward actions?

James 1:23–25 describes people who have become believers but who also continue living their old lives of sin. They listen and hear the word of God, but instead of practicing what they've learned, they do not apply it. Some believers today are guilty of the same thing. The world tells us that it doesn't really matter what scripture teaches as long as we're living good, decent lives—but this is false, and if we buy into this lie, we are deceiving ourselves.

READ JAMES 1:26–27.

11. List the three instructions James gives to believers.

READ EPHESIANS 4:29–32.

12. What instructions does Paul give believers?

James and Paul offer believers similar advice for how they ought to live their lives. But James makes it clear that before this can happen, believers need to study God's word and let it take root. Only then can we be rid of the old self and, as Paul describes, adopt the righteous and holy lives God has in mind for us.

❁ SOMETHING TO THINK ABOUT: REAL CHANGE THROUGH RESPONSE

Scripture is filled with examples of rewards or consequences associated with listening and acting to the word of God. For instance, the prophet Jonah was sent to Nineveh to warn the people of God's impending judgment on their nation (Jonah 1–4). The people of Nineveh listened to what Jonah had to say and responded with action. Because they *responded* to what they heard—by turning from their evil ways—God had compassion on them and did not destroy their nation.

Responding to what we hear and learn about God is key to living a pure and righteous life. Both James and Paul teach that it's our response to God's teaching that equips and prepares us, for the road ahead. Just like the people of Nineveh, we need to hear, listen, and above all, take action.

If we truly seek a relationship with God, then it's imperative that we apply our faith to our lives. It's not enough to go to church and hear a sermon or to read our Bibles and know God's truths; it's only by putting into practice what we hear and learn that our attitudes and behaviors will change, and with this change comes the confidence that our faith is real, alive, and active.

4

Overcoming Prejudice Behavior

James 2:1–13

✿ SUMMARY

In the last few verses, James instructed everyone to not only hear the teachings of Scripture, but also to do what they say. Here James adds a further clarification: when we do these things, we should do them equally, to the benefit of everyone. In other words, the church should not give anyone preferential treatment or be prejudiced against some of its members. Instead, *everyone* should be afforded the full privilege that comes with faith in Christ.

James wants the church to understand that it should treat all believers with equal respect regardless of their backgrounds. He reminds them of the royal law, "Love your neighbor as yourself," which they had previously heard but failed to practice.

Although both the rich and poor attended the same church meetings, the church wrongly focused all their attention on the needs of the wealthy while at the same time ignoring and disrespecting the poor. James points out this error and reminds them that by breaking the law, even by the slightest fraction, they are guilty of breaking the whole law.

❈ GETTING THE BASICS

READ JAMES 2:1–5.

1. How was the church treating the wealthy?

2. How was the church treating the poor?

READ 1 TIMOTHY 6:17–19.

3. How can wealth affect a person's spirituality?

REREAD JAMES 2:5.

4. What does God promise all believers regardless of their wealth or poverty?

READ GALATIANS 3:26–29.

5. What is the common factor that unites diverse believers?

6. If all believers are heirs of God's promise, how important is personal wealth?

Both James and Paul teach that believers, regardless of their outward appearance or earthly possessions, have a spiritual wealth that comes from God. Because of that spiritual wealth, and because all believers are heirs to God's promises, everyone should be treated with the same respect, whether they are rich or poor, healthy or sick, man or woman. In fact, we are to value all believers as fellow heirs, as important to God and to the church—no matter their earthly station. With these instructions, both James and Paul—who have stressed the importance of *applying* the word of God to our actions—are also telling us that when we do act, we need to act without favoritism, without prejudice. Our behavior is to be godly at all times, with all people.

DIGGING DEEPER

READ JAMES 2:8–11.

7. James confronts the church about their behavior by quoting the law. What part of the law have they broken by playing favorites?

8. Why is breaking this small part of the law taken so seriously?

READ ROMANS 3:20.

9. According to Paul, what can the law reveal to us?

READ ROMANS 13:8–10.

10. To correct our behavior, avoid sin, and fulfill the law, what core commandment do we need to uphold?

Paul teaches that the law can reveal sin to us. The law itself doesn't correct our behavior, but it does show how our behavior falls short. In Matthew 22:37–40, Jesus taught us how to correct our behavior: "Love the Lord your God with all your heart and with all your soul and with all your mind. This is the first and greatest commandment. And the second is like it: Love your neighbor as yourself. All the Law and the Prophets hang on these two commandments."

At the time, Jesus was speaking to Jews, but notice that he didn't specify our neighbors as Jews only, thereby excluding everyone else. Rather, he commanded people to display unbiased love to *all* people, Jew or Gentile, believer or unbeliever. He didn't leave any loopholes for favoritism.

Now, when addressing the church, both James and Paul are reinforcing this command. Believers are not to play favorites, or they will be held accountable for breaking God's law. Instead believers need to love everyone, and that love needs to be demonstrated through their actions. This is just as important for us to apply today.

11. In light of the instruction to love everyone, how should the church treat people?

12. How does love fulfill both the moral and social responsibilities of believers?

READ JAMES 2:12–13.

13. What does James say believers can expect if they do not show love and mercy to *all* people?

14. If the church showed love and mercy to all people, what kind of effect could that have in our communities?

✸ SOMETHING TO THINK ABOUT: ACCEPTING OTHERS

Individually, we can apply love and mercy on our own to improve the way we treat people, but James wasn't writing to an individual. He was writing to a church that neglected to treat all believers as equals and heirs to God's promise. So it's not enough for individuals to display love and mercy—the entire church must. But not all churches welcome all people, and that's the point of this chapter. It shouldn't matter what sins a person has committed in the past or whether they are "holy enough" to attend church. God offers salvation to all people regardless of their background.

To carry out this command effectively, it's up to the church to accept, love, and care for everyone who wants to be a part of God's kingdom. Acceptance is important, because without it, divisions within the church can make the church less effective in carrying out God's mission. Unity within a church allows its believers to better coordinate outreach activities, better minister to others, and better honor God.

The church must unite with one another and accept all people, just as Jesus did. Unity is not found in a master plan drawn up by men, but rather found when we believe, teach, and practice what scripture tells us. Imagine the effect we can have on this world if all believers *worldwide* expressed their Christian faith by loving and accepting all people—just like God loves and accepts us. This, as Paul said, would be the fulfillment of the law—something we should be striving for every day.

The alternative is much worse. James makes it clear that mercy will be shown to those of us who love with mercy, but he also says mercy will not be shown to those of us who don't show it to others. So while our actions ought to reflect love and mercy to bring about great things in our communities, it is also a core responsibility of believers—with severe consequences if we fail to take that responsibility seriously.

5

The Role of Faith and Works

James 2:14–26

❈ SUMMARY

In this chapter, James continues explaining the important connection between faith and works. He tells his readers that it's not good enough to just *say* you have faith; if you are not *acting* on that faith, your faith is dead and useless.

Expanding on the principle that believers ought to do good equally to *all* people, James writes specifically about those deeds we ought to do. A person who acts out their faith in the form of good deeds understands the difference between *knowing* the truth and *living* the truth. Just saying you have faith is not enough because faith without deeds might as well not be there. Faith must be backed by actions that are consistent with that faith—proof that a transformation has taken place in the heart of a believer.

❊ GETTING THE BASICS

READ JAMES 2:14.

1. What kind of a person is James talking about in this verse?

READ JAMES 2:15–17.

2. In what way does the well-wisher in these verses demonstrate he has a dead and useless faith?

READ JAMES 2:18–20.

3. How does James say a person shows their faith?

4. What point is James making when he says that even demons believe there's one God?

James is talking about people who say they have faith but don't want the responsibility of doing godly things. To illustrate this, James provides an example of a man who sees his neighbor in need but does nothing to help, except to wish him well. James teaches that the man's well-wishing means nothing to the one who is suffering—his words are empty because they aren't followed by action. James also makes a startling comparison in these verses between demons and a person who doesn't demonstrate their faith for others to see. He basically says, "So you believe in one God? Big deal! Even the demons know that! If that's all there is to your faith, you're no different from them!" He tells his readers that acknowledging the existence of God is useless if a person doesn't practice what he believes. In the same way, a faith that isn't followed by action is the same as the well-wisher's words: meaningless and empty.

READ ROMANS 3:21–22 AND EPHESIANS 2:8–9.

5. According to Paul, how does a person receive salvation?

6. What does *not* earn a person salvation?

READ PHILIPPIANS 3:4–6.

7. Here Paul describes his religious attitude and lifestyle before he became a Christian, back when he was still a part of the Jewish establishment. What kinds of "good works" did Paul do as a way of earning God's approval?

READ PHILIPPIANS 3:7–9.

8. Why does Paul consider his heritage, good works, and religious zeal as pointless and useless?

9. What was missing from Paul's religious lifestyle before his conversion?

Paul repeatedly emphasizes that we are not justified by works in any way. In his ministry, Paul dealt a lot with religious legalism—the idea that salvation comes only by following religious law—and he used his message of the free gift of salvation to debunk this way of thinking. Paul taught that a person is not entitled to salvation just by keeping to a set of rules and regulations (as he himself had been taught), and it's only through faith in Jesus Christ that a person is found justified in the eyes of God.

Isn't this interesting? James appears to be saying one thing (your faith must have works), and Paul another (works mean nothing).

❊ DIGGING DEEPER

REREAD JAMES 2:14, 16, AND 20.

10. What kinds of people is James confronting in these verses and what does he accuse them of?

READ GALATIANS 2:15–16; 5:4.

11. What kinds of people is Paul confronting in these verses and what does he accuse them of?

Both James and Paul were dealing with different types of people with regards to faith. While James's audience was in fact believers, they were nonetheless trying to get out of doing good works. On the other hand, Paul's audience, who were also believers, focused solely on abiding by a set of religious rules—in other words, they were doing good works because they were told to, but were neglecting their faith.

So one reason why it appears that James and Paul are saying two different things is because they are addressing two different types of people. James was tailoring his message to one group (the people who weren't doing any good), and Paul was tailoring his message to another (the people who didn't have any substantial faith).

READ JAMES 2:21–22.

12. What two things were working together that made Abraham's faith complete?

READ JAMES 2:23–26.

13. What do these verses tell us about the importance of faith and the way faith is expressed?

READ EPHESIANS 2:10 AND 1 TIMOTHY 6:18.

14. What do these verses tell us about Paul and good works?

READ 1 THESSALONIANS 1:3 AND 2 THESSALONIANS 1:11.

15. What does Paul teach as the prompting behind every good deed?

READ GALATIANS 5:6.

16. What does Paul teach as the only thing of value to a person, and how is it expressed?

REREAD JAMES 2:17, 26.

17. Keeping in mind Paul's teachings about faith, action, love, and salvation, how would you sum up what James is teaching about faith and works in these two verses?

Because both James and Paul were dealing with different audiences, it was important to explain the relationship between faith and works specifically to the people who were reading their letters. James focused on those who claimed to have faith but who failed to demonstrate that faith to others. Paul, on the other hand, was more focused on those who kept to a strict set of rules instead of relying on their faith. And although James emphasizes how works are related to faith, and Paul stresses how faith is related to salvation, there is no contradiction. Both men realized how important actions *and* faith are to a believer's life and salvation—not as things separate and independent from one another, but joined together in the heart of all true believers.

❊ SOMETHING TO THINK ABOUT: GENUINE FAITH

Imitation faith was a real danger to the early church, and many letters in the New Testament confront this issue head on. And just like the people of the early church, modern believers risk deluding themselves into thinking they have genuine faith when in fact, they do not.

Genuine faith means accepting Jesus Christ as lord and savior and acting on that belief. It's not enough to *say* we believe; without acting on that belief, we risk being the mere *listeners* that James warns us about.

This is what Jesus says about those who only *verbally* acknowledge him: "Why do you call me, 'Lord, Lord,' and do not do what I say?" (Luke 6:46). And again: "Not everyone who says to me, 'Lord, Lord,' will enter the kingdom of heaven, but only he who does the will of my Father who is in heaven" (Matthew 7:21). Jesus insisted that a person's faith must produce acts of obedience, and that's the exact point James is making in his letter. Paul also understands the importance of having a true and living faith and gives believers a specific set of instructions: "Examine yourselves to see whether you are in the faith; test yourselves. Don't you realize that Christ Jesus is in you—unless, of course, you fail the test?" (2 Corinthians 13:5).

But how do we go about testing our faith? James provides the answer: by examining what we do. If we allow our faith to be expressed in what we do, we have proof that a transformation has taken place and a real and deep faith has taken root. In other words, genuine faith produces good deeds as well as obedient actions—and this is taught by James, Paul, and even Jesus himself.

Once we understand genuine faith, our "good works" will take on new meaning—not as things done to earn God's favor, but as things done to display our gratitude, our transformation, and our sincerity as believers.

Our faith is what saves us and that salvation is by faith alone. We need to stop pretending we can "earn" God's favor and let our good works be evidence of the faith that saved us.

Remember, it's faith, salvation, and good works all working together for the glory of God.

6

The Power of Words

James 3:1–12

❖ SUMMARY

Up to this point, James has taught the correct way for us to act when it comes to temptation, trials, prejudices, works, and faith. But here he goes further: it's not just what you *do*, but even what you *say*.

Because oral teaching was common during this time in history, James uses teachers as examples of people whose words have a profound impact on others. But teachers aren't the only people whose words matter: every believer is equally responsible for exercising and controlling their own speech. James also adds that once a person has gained control over what he says, he is better able to control other areas of his life.

❉ GETTING THE BASICS

READ JAMES 3:1–5.

1. Why do you think James says teachers will be judged more strictly?

2. James mentions bits in the mouths of horses and rudders on a ship. What purpose do these objects serve?

3. What is James trying to say when he uses those illustrations?

4. Describe a time when your words have steered another person, for good or for bad.

James says that teachers will be judged more strictly for their words, probably because of the influence they have over others. Words, after all, have the same power as rudders—they can steer our lives and the lives of other people. And we all have affected other people with our words before. Although here James is speaking specifically to teachers, *all* believers affect the people around them by what they say. And so we all should heed his warning: words matter.

READ TITUS 2:6–8.

5. What does Paul say we should do with our words?

READ EPHESIANS 4:29.

6. What should our words be doing?

REREAD JAMES 2:15–16.

7. Here James gives an example of someone saying "the right things." According to James and Paul, how is this not enough?

READ EPHESIANS 5:6–7.

8. How does God respond to deceitful and empty words?

Controlling the tongue can be difficult, but it's imperative for believers to understand the impact that God wants our words to have. Both James and Paul teach that our words should benefit the people around us. James stresses that our words can steer people in the right direction. Paul stresses that our words should build people up. By carefully choosing the words we use, we can focus on making a positive impact wherever we are.

❊ DIGGING DEEPER

READ JAMES 3:5–6.

9.   What can the tongue do that makes it so dangerous?

10. Since our words can corrupt the whole person, what danger is there in not controlling what we say?

Reread James 3:2.

11. If we are able to control our words, what is in store for us?

Read Romans 3:23.

12. According to Paul, will we ever achieve perfection?

Read James 3:7–8.

13. According to James, what's the one thing man can never tame?

First, James points out how important our words are. Then, together with Paul, we get an idea about what our words should be doing. Here, James makes it known that controlling our words will be a lifelong struggle. It's something we should always be aware of, and we should always strive for improvement. Consider this: when James wrote this letter, man was taming all kinds of animals. Now think about where we are in history today: mankind has spread to all corners of the world, continued taming animals, made deserts beautiful and green, molded minerals and resources into vast and tall buildings—and even now, we have yet to tame our tongues. It's not only a struggle throughout our entire lives, but through our entire history.

READ JAMES 3:9–12.

14. What two things does James say we're doing?

15. James points out that men have been made in God's likeness. With that in mind, do you think that by cursing man—or cursing at them, or wishing them harm—we're actually insulting God? Explain.

16. What does James imply we ought to be doing with our words?

READ ROMANS 10:10 AND 1 THESSALONIANS 5:16–18.

17. What are some ways we can use our words to praise God?

James has pointed out that believers mostly do two things with their words: praise God and curse each other. He is emphasizing here that those two things are at odds, completely incompatible, and unacceptable. On the other hand, Paul gives us excellent examples of how we *should* be using our words as believers. We should focus on doing *those* things, and while we certainly won't reach perfection, we can certainly improve our walk with God.

❋ SOMETHING TO THINK ABOUT: AWARENESS AND STRUGGLE WITH WORDS

James understood the power of words, and he cautions his readers to exercise control when they're speaking. He points out that a person who can control what he says is better able to control other areas of his Christian life—a clear teaching that connects what we say with righteous, Christian living. We need to be mindful not only of our rash words, but also of the empty words that are useless to those in need.

But interestingly, James doesn't give us any easy solutions. He points out how destructive our words can be, but there's no easy way to fix the problem. So what is James getting at with all this talk?

James knows that making people *aware* of the problem is the first and most important part of correcting bad behavior. We need to first be aware of *what* we're saying and what it is we *should* be saying, and that puts us in a better position to actually build people up with our words. This will ultimately lead us to the behavior God desires.

7

True Wisdom

James 3:13–18

❀ SUMMARY

In the previous chapters, James laid the groundwork for what he talks about here. He's already told us that our Christian faith is demonstrated to others by our attitudes, our behaviors, and even our speech, but now, he's going to talk about two kinds of wisdom—godly wisdom and worldly wisdom.

James describes both kinds of wisdom, and begins by telling us that worldly wisdom is something that motivates us to only think about ourselves and our own desires. It's a self-centered and selfish attitude and produces nothing but disorder and all kinds of confusion.

Godly wisdom, on the other hand, is something that motivates us to think of others before ourselves. In fact, James has been describing this kind of wisdom all along in his letter, with his teachings about correct Christian attitudes and actions. But here, he labels this motivation as godly wisdom and makes it clear that it's expressed through unselfish attitudes and behaviors.

❄ GETTING THE BASICS

READ JAMES 3:13.

1. What question does James ask in his opening verse?

2. How does James say a person shows their wisdom and understanding?

3. How does James say good works should be demonstrated?

Humility is an attitude that's absent of conceit, self-interest, and ambition. And it's not just an inward attitude; *demonstrating* humility to others is just as important as having a humble attitude. This is something James will come back to later.

READ JAMES 3:14–16.

4. How does James characterize worldly wisdom, and what does it lead to?

READ 1 CORINTHIANS 3:3.

5. What kind of behavior were the Corinthians displaying that caused Paul to call them worldly?

READ EPHESIANS 2:1–3.

6.   How does Paul connect worldly wisdom with our old nature?

James makes the point that worldly wisdom is defined by self-ishness and a commitment to our own self-interest. But this only leads to chaos in our lives, disagreements with the people around us, and frustration in our faith. Likewise, Paul links selfishness with worldly wisdom, but he goes even further. He also connects our old nature—from before we were saved—with worldly wisdom, telling us that worldly wisdom should be a thing of the past for those who are in Christ.

✸ DIGGING DEEPER

READ JAMES 3:17.

7.   How does James describe the wisdom that comes from God?

READ COLOSSIANS 3:12–15.

8. How do Paul's instructions to believers relate to the godly wisdom described by James?

READ PHILIPPIANS 2:3–4.

9. How does Paul say humility is demonstrated?

10. How is godly wisdom and acts of humility connected?

Both James and Paul agree that godly wisdom motivates believers to outwardly display the right kind of conduct to all people. This includes having integrity with others (purity), refusing to entice anger in other people (peace loving), placing value on other people's feelings (considerate, submissive), forgiving the mistakes of others (mercy), treating others equally (impartial), and wholeheartedly caring about other people's welfare (sincere). In other words, if we're motivated by godly wisdom, we'll stop acting with only our own best interest in mind and instead, we'll take to heart the concerns and needs of others.

READ JAMES 3:18.

11. What does James mean when he says, "Peacemakers who sow in peace raise a harvest of righteousness?"

READ EPHESIANS 4:1–3.

12. What behaviors does Paul list that will help us to live a life of righteousness?

The qualities described by James and Paul in this chapter are things every Christian should aspire to. It's only when a believer adopts this way of thinking—godly wisdom—that he can act appropriately and behave the way Paul and James are encouraging believers to behave. And that behavior will result in righteousness, or a righteous life.

So James gives us the answer to his opening question, "Who is wise and understanding?" It's the person who places others before himself in everything he does. That is the basis for the conduct that God expects from us. Having godly wisdom means knowing that everything we do should be done with humility, with others in mind.

✦ SOMETHING TO THINK ABOUT: ARE WE SERVING OURSELVES OR OTHERS?

James describes a lot of qualities that are a part of godly wisdom. Taken together, these qualities—like humility, mercy, and gentleness—create a spirit of selflessness and allow us to put others before ourselves. That selflessness should be the goal we all have as believers. And Jesus is our ultimate model, because with complete selflessness, he gave himself up for us.

But achieving and acting on selflessness can be difficult. Often, we have such a hard time giving up that worldly wisdom that we held to before we were believers. So we must be aware, at all times, of what we're doing and why. We need to always question whether we're acting out of our own self-interest or in the welfare of others. Almost always, if the answer is that we're acting in our own self-interest, then it's the wrong act.

Remember the example in James 2:15–17 about a person who was in need? The response from the believer was, "Go, I wish you well; keep warm and well fed." James told us this was a problem. Although the believer used kind words to the one who was suffering, his words meant absolutely nothing because they weren't sincere. And we know they weren't sincere because they weren't backed by any action. Absolutely nothing was done to alleviate the suffering of the person in need. Why should this be considered a selfish response? Because the believer *held onto something* (money, a jacket, whatever) for himself rather than giving it to address the needs of others. He placed himself before other people.

8

Submission

James 4:1–10

❈ SUMMARY

James just described worldly and godly wisdom, and here he explains why having the right wisdom is so important. He makes it clear that chaos and conflict are the direct result of our own selfishness. He wants us to realize that by looking after our own self-interests—as the world would have us do—we are only further separating ourselves from God.

But James offers us a way out: we must return to God by submitting to him. In effect, James is telling us that we're powerless by ourselves, completely unable to achieve godly wisdom on our own, unable to nurture selflessness in our lives. But if we submit to God, if we make certain our relationship with God is pure and true, we can resist the wisdom of the world and find peace.

James's teachings in this chapter should prompt us to look intently at who we are, cause us to question which wisdom we're following, and provoke us into resubmitting our lives to God.

✸ GETTING THE BASICS

READ JAMES 4:1–3.

1. According to James, what causes conflicts in our lives?

2. James says sometimes we want something but don't get it. How can this create conflict in our own lives?

3. In what way is selfishness the driving force behind conflicts?

READ 1 CORINTHIANS 3:3.

4. What does Paul say is the direct cause of jealousy and conflicts?

READ ROMANS 8:5–8.

5. In verse 5, Paul talks about living according to the sinful nature and according to the spirit. How is this similar to having worldly wisdom and godly wisdom?

6. What does Paul mean when he says those who live with the sinful nature "have their minds set on what that nature desires"?

7. How does Paul describe the mind that is controlled by the spirit?

A conflict is when two or more people want different things. For instance, a child who wants more freedom and a parent who is reluctant to give that freedom; or two politicians who say terrible things about each other because they both want to be elected. And that's exactly what James is talking about here. He says that anyone who adheres to worldly wisdom will struggle with conflict because worldly wisdom encourages people to try to get whatever they want. And because sometimes two or more people want the same thing but can't all have it, conflict results. In other words, many of the sinful behaviors we see in life—like fighting, yelling, and lying—are symptoms of a heart that's focused on selfishness, the driving force behind conflict. Paul agrees, but he adds even more: he says that someone who lives according to the Spirit—or who has godly wisdom—will have life and, importantly, *peace*.

READ JAMES 4:4–6.

8. To James, having worldly wisdom is like being "friends with the world." How does being a friend of the world affect our relationship with God?

9. What does it mean to become an enemy of God?

James says that a person is either God's friend or God's enemy. There is no middle ground. A person cannot claim to be a believer while at the same time following a world that's hostile to God. Jesus talked about this same subject in Matthew 6:24, saying, "No one can serve two masters. Either he will hate the one and love the other, or he will be devoted to the one and despise the other." Either we embrace God or we embrace the world. We can't have it both ways.

✹ DIGGING DEEPER

READ JAMES 4:7–8.

10. If we want to reject friendship with the world, reject worldly wisdom, and accept godly wisdom, what do we need to do?

REREAD ROMANS 8:7.

11. How does Paul describe our sinful natures?

READ ROMANS 6:11–14.

12. What do these verses imply about submission?

13. What are some ways that believers can submit to God?

James tells us to stop behaving in a worldly manner and instead, behave in a godly manner. Sometimes we think we can do this on our own, but we can't (as Paul clearly tells us), and we have to stop thinking we can. James tells us that it's only by submitting our lives to God's authority that we can end our reliance on worldly wisdom. And Paul confirms it, by describing submission as an act of humble obedience, where we turn away from our own selfish desires and give God complete control over our lives.

READ JAMES 4:9–10.

14. Why do you think James tells us to grieve, mourn, and wail over our sinful actions?

15. How do you think this relates to submission?

READ 2 CORINTHIANS 7:10.

16. What is the benefit of having godly sorrow?

17. James tells us that if we humble ourselves, God will lift us up. Why is humility so important when it comes to submission to God?

18. How can we display humility to God?

The opposite of humility is pride. When we believe we have all the right answers in our lives—or when we don't look for God's guidance in our lives—we are in effect telling God that we don't need, want, or trust his wisdom. And it's this kind of pride that causes us to act selfishly, ignoring God as well as the needs of others. But this is wrong and damages the relationship between a believer and God. When a believer recognizes the severity of his sin, repents, and admits that God's wisdom is the correct wisdom—only then can he demonstrate the ultimate act of humility by willingly submitting and surrendering his life to God.

❖ SOMETHING TO THINK ABOUT: REAL CHANGE

When a person truly submits to God, a real change takes place in their lives. No longer do they conform to worldly standards, but instead they focus on godly standards. But too many believers today compromise God's standards for the world's standards, and James says this is wrong.

The world says it's okay to be greedy, that it's okay to look out for number one. After all, if a person doesn't look out for himself, who will? And we all know the world is like this because there's true suffering everywhere: hunger, homelessness, and despair.

But if people really took to heart what God teaches, they'd look out for one another and the needs of each other would be a priority. But this isn't happening. Why? Because the world is hostile to God. And people follow this hostility because it feeds into their greed and selfishness. They're more interested in what they can get here and now than in their eternal future. And in their pursuit of selfishness and greed, others get hurt. Others pay the price. It's this kind of attitude that makes people enemies of God.

And if we do these same things, how can we claim to be believers? Aren't we to be different and set apart? Shouldn't the world see God through us, through our actions? If we behave the way the world would have us behave, we haven't shown any change to others and we contribute to the world's mockery of God and his truth. That's right; *we make a mockery of God.*

As believers, we need to make a choice. We can either be God's friend and live according to his truths, or we can be God's enemy and live according to the world's truths. We can't have it both ways, and if we try, God will spit us from his mouth for our indecisiveness (Revelation 3:16).

So instead of just saying we've changed, let's do what's necessary to *really change*. Let's submit to God and give *him* true control over our lives. Let's apply *his* wisdom, do away with our selfishness, and focus on the needs of others. Only then can we have peace. Only then have we really changed.

9

God's Role

James 4:11–17

❈ SUMMARY

James has already explained how our selfishness gets in the way of our submission to God. But selfishness doesn't only damage our relationship with God—it also damages our relationships with other people.

To illustrate this, James mentions two types of behavior that we're all familiar with: judging others, and making plans for our lives. He explains that because we lack God's power and authority, we're actually unqualified to do either of these things. Only God can pass a fair and impartial judgment, and only God can decide what's in store for our future. James reminds us that we have no business trying to take on God's role.

But sometimes we do disregard that truth, and we sometimes judge others and make plans as though we are in charge of our futures. When we do that, we are actually ignoring God's authority and demonstrating our unwillingness to submit to him. Even worse, when we prioritize our desires over God's will, we inadvertently make the claim that we are more important than he is. And there isn't anything more inaccurate—or more dangerous—than that.

❈ GETTING THE BASICS

READ JAMES 4:11–12.

1. What behavior does James tell us not to do?

2. What does James say we are guilty of doing when we slander or judge another person?

REREAD JAMES 2:8.

3. What law is James referring to?

READ ROMANS 13:10 AND 1 CORINTHIANS 16:14.

4.   What does Paul say every believer *should* be expressing?

READ GALATIANS 5:13–15.

5.   What does Paul warn about if we don't show love to each other?

James again directs our attention to the royal law. But this time, instead of explaining what the law is as he did in chapter 2, he tells us exactly how we're breaking it: by judging and slandering others. Both James and Paul teach that *love* should be displayed in all our actions. But when we judge and slander one another, love is not being demonstrated—we are being disobedient to God and breaking his law.

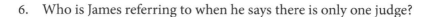

REREAD JAMES 4:12.

6. Who is James referring to when he says there is only one judge?

7. According to James, what is God able to do in his role as judge?

James says that God is the only one qualified to judge others. Why? Because only he has the power to save and destroy. In other words, God can condemn a man for wrongdoing, but God can also be merciful and provide reconciliation. It's the same way with us as believers: God can condemn us for our sin, but he can also provide a way to salvation.

Back in Galatians 5:13–15, Paul tells us that people have the power to *destroy*—but nowhere in scripture does it say people have the power to *save*. When we place ourselves in the role of judge, the only thing we're able to do is destroy one another. We're great at condemnation, but our limitations as humans prevent us from offering anyone salvation. But not so with God. The only sensible thing to do is what James clearly instructs: leave judgment to God.

8. In what way does judging others show a lack of submission to God?

✾ DIGGING DEEPER

READ JAMES 4:13–17.

9. How are we limited when we make future plans?

10. What point is James making when he tells us that we don't know the future and that our lives are fleeting?

11. Since we lack the capacity to make and enforce our own plans, what should we depend on to guide our activities?

READ ACTS 18:20–21, ROMANS 15:32, AND 1 CORINTHIANS 16:7.

12. What can we learn from Paul when making plans for the future?

It isn't future planning or future goals that James is condemning here; it's the *way* we plan. When we bypass God and make our own decisions, we arrogantly assume we know the best course for our lives. But we don't have the ability to make that determination because our knowledge of the future is limited. Just like Paul, we need to depend on God and his will when making our plans, because our lives are so uncertain and out of our control.

Reread James 4:16.

13. Why does James calls our plans "arrogant schemes"?

14. According to James, when we make plans about our lives without involving God, we reveal our own arrogance. When we do so, whose authority are we trusting for our lives—God's or ours?

15. Whose authority should we be trusting?

16. Why would boasting about our plans be considered evil?

REREAD JAMES 4:15.

17. James gives us an example of how we ought to make plans for our lives. Why is this a good example to follow?

18. In what way does making our own plans for the future demonstrate a lack of submission to God?

James teaches that we need to use God's will to guide us when making future plans because if we don't, we're sinning. How? Because every time we brag about the plans we've made on our own, without consulting God, we're claiming an authority in our lives that God should have. Living by our own authority demonstrates that we don't want, need, or desire God's input in any of our decisions. But by laying aside our own self-interests and instead relying on God's guidance for all our decisions, we're not only submitting to God's authority, but also cultivating the kind of godly wisdom James has been talking about throughout his letter. And Paul provides plenty of examples of going before God and relying on his will before deciding what to do.

❁ SOMETHING TO THINK ABOUT: LOOKING AT OURSELVES

James gives us a lot to consider about judging others. Often our judgments are wrong and unfair. Why? Because our judgment can be motivated by jealousy, pride, anger, or ambition; our judgment creates conflict and damages relationships. As James teaches, we are in no position to judge another person's actions or motives because we are not God. It really is that simple. We lack God's ability to save the people we judge, and we are unequipped to offer a fair and discerning judgment of the heart. He's the only one who can judge fairly.

Nothing reveals a heart full of arrogance, pride, or conceit more clearly than judging another person. And when we do this, we aren't obeying God's law of love; instead, we're placing ourselves in God's position and, in effect, considering ourselves to be God's equal!

The story of Jesus and the woman caught in adultery (John 8:1–11) is a perfect example of what James is teaching here. Jesus responded to the woman's accusers with, "If any of you is without sin, let him be the first to throw a stone at her." Or, in other words, "You want to be judges? Fine. If any of you are qualified like God is qualified, feel free to start judging." But once we do, then we've unequivocally declared ourselves to be God's equal—a sin of pride and arrogance if there ever was one.

This does not mean that we are not supposed to see sin for what it is. Just as with the woman caught in adultery, we should recognize sin when we see it. We should understand what actions are wrong and sinful, should know what actions need to be avoided in our own lives. But we should not *judge* a person who has sinned, because that person should be judged by God alone.

If our behavior and attitudes toward a person change because that person has sinned, we're in dangerous territory. Because the response we *should* have, as James teaches, is simply to love that person, just as we should love all people, even when someone does the wrong thing. Jesus did exactly that when he was presented with the adulterous woman.

Let's follow his example.

10

Maintaining Faith, Patience, and Endurance

James 5:1–12

❧ SUMMARY

James just told us to submit to God's authority, and that includes putting aside our own self-interests and no longer judging others. But if submission means *not* doing certain things, what things are we to do? Here he explains that we're to be righteous and patient in all circumstances.

We can't use our own personal hardships as an excuse to judge others or disregard correct godly behavior. By trusting God and persevering through hardship and suffering, we demonstrate our willingness to give God control over all our circumstances; that's exactly what submission to God is all about.

✤ GETTING THE BASICS

READ JAMES 5:1–6.

1. How do we know that God is aware of the terrible things people are doing?

REREAD JAMES 3:13–18.

2. How can we avoid becoming the terrible people James describes in these verses?

READ 2 CORINTHIANS 5:10.

3. We already know that God will judge evil people for their deeds, but what can we expect in our own judgment?

READ ROMANS 2:11 AND COLOSSIANS 3:25.

4. How do we know that God will judge everyone's actions—including believers?

Being a believer doesn't automatically exclude us from God's judgment. As a result, we have to guard ourselves against corruption. God tells us not to show favoritism because in doing so we break the royal law. So of course God himself would not show favoritism in his judgment, because why would he break his own law? Instead, he will judge, hold accountable, and respond to everyone's actions—including those of believers.

READ ROMANS 12:17 AND 21.

5. What does Paul say is the correct response when we are suffering at the hands of others?

READ EPHESIANS 6:14–18.

6. How do you think we can overcome evil with good?

READ EPHESIANS 6:8 AND COLOSSIANS 3:23–24.

7. According to Paul, what will believers receive if they overcome evil with good?

God expects believers to demonstrate a high level of conduct and character that's equal to the character of Christ, and he expects this in every situation. Although it can be extremely difficult to respond to evil with kindness, it's our godly character that sets us apart from others and brings glory to God. And this godly character is obtained only through our submission to God.

❀ DIGGING DEEPER

READ JAMES 5:7–12.

8. How does James tell us we should be living our lives every day?

REREAD JAMES 1:3 AND 2 THESSALONIANS 1:3–4.

9. Paul commends the Thessalonians for their faith and patience while enduring persecution. How are faith and perseverance connected?

READ PHILIPPIANS 2:13–15.

10. Both James and Paul tell us it's wrong to grumble and complain. How are these actions connected to self-interest and lack of patience?

Complaining shows a lack of perseverance and perseverance is supposed to come from faith. So when we complain, we're really revealing that we lack the faith that God will take care of us. This also means we're not submitting to God's power. After all, if we had faith, and if we were submitting to God's plan and his will, we would have no reason to complain. It's all related: perseverance is directly tied to our faith, and it's our faith that's made stronger through our submission to God.

REREAD JAMES 5:10–11.

11. Who should we look to for examples of endurance while suffering?

READ JOB 1:13–22 AND 2:7–10.

12. How does Job respond to his suffering?

READ 2 CORINTHIANS 12:9–10.

13. How does Paul respond to his suffering?

The prophets James refers to in these verses could also include Jeremiah, Ezekiel, Daniel, Hosea, Amos, and Isaiah. These Old Testament prophets suffered abuse and persecution because they spoke openly about sin and repentance. They persevered through their suffering and abuses because they had faith in God and submitted to his will. We must look to their examples and do the same.

READ 2 CORINTHIANS 1:3–7.

14. According to Paul, God comforts us through our troubles. If we want to follow God's example, how should we respond when we see others in trouble?

15. What does Paul say this comfort produces?

REREAD JAMES 3:17.

16. The qualities James mentions in this verse, attainable through submission to God, will naturally compel us to comfort others. How does demonstrating these qualities reveal the kind of relationship we have with God?

Scripture tells us it's our responsibility to encourage and comfort one another because doing so provides spiritual strength, deepens faith, and creates unity among believers. And being able to offer encouragement and comfort will emerge naturally if our relationship with God is correct. By submitting our lives to God and allowing his character and qualities to guide us, we'll be better able to push our own self-interests aside and concentrate on the needs of others.

❈ SOMETHING TO THINK ABOUT: ACCOUNTABILITY REGARDLESS OF CIRCUMSTANCE

Scripture provides numerous examples of Old Testament believers—including Noah, Moses, and David—who continued in their faith despite suffering extreme hardship and persecution. But Paul's life offers us some great lessons to learn, too.

Throughout his letters, Paul describes his life as one filled with difficulties and complications. For example, he tells us that he experienced periods of hunger, thirst, nakedness, weariness, physical pain, and imprisonment (2 Corinthians 11:23–28), and he even described himself as being full of fear and trembling (1 Corinthians 2:3). But he also told us that he drew strength from each terrible circumstance he faced (2 Corinthians 12:10) and understood that it was God who was in control of his life. Although God allowed Paul to undergo extreme circumstances in his lifetime, Paul was convinced he'd be rewarded for his faith and perseverance—if not here on earth, certainly in eternity (2 Timothy 4:8).

The same is true for us today. Once we submit to God as Paul did and acknowledge that our faith lies in God and God alone, correct godly actions will follow no matter what kind of situation we face. Our motivation for continued submission to God, as well as displaying correct godly behavior, shouldn't be conditional on what's happening in our lives. Therefore, we have no excuse for ungodly behavior. Our motivation should be to please God and live a life that displays godly wisdom—even when we're suffering—because God will hold us accountable regardless of our circumstances.

11

Submission Through Prayer

James 5:13–20

❀ SUMMARY

James closes his letter with a discussion of prayer. He teaches that no matter our circumstances, good or bad, we need to be in continuous communication with God. Our submission to God's power and authority is demonstrated by prayer, and it can result in great changes in our lives and in the lives of others. By praying to God on behalf of other people, we're also practicing the command to love others as ourselves; this exhibits the selflessness that we gain by submitting to God and shows we have gained godly wisdom.

❋ GETTING THE BASICS

READ JAMES 5:13–15.

1. James provides us with several examples of when prayer is appropriate—when we're in trouble, when we're happy, and when we're sick. What does this teach us about praying?

READ EPHESIANS 6:18.

2. What does this verse teach about the freedom we have in prayer?

READ 1 THESSALONIANS 5:17–18.

3. In what way does following Paul's instructions in these verses display our submission to God's authority?

Everything in our lives, whether good or bad, is under the power and authority of God. And by acknowledging his power and authority in prayer, we demonstrate our submission to him. There isn't a right or wrong time for submission—submission to God is an everyday, every moment necessity, no matter our circumstances. And this is best demonstrated by praying to God every day, at any moment, no matter our circumstances.

READ JAMES 5:16–18.

4.   What two things does James say believers should do for each other?

READ EPHESIANS 3:14–19.

5.   In these verses, we have an example of Paul praying for the needs of others. How is this act related to selflessness and submission to God?

REREAD JAMES 5:16.

6. How do you think confession and prayer can lead to physical and spiritual healing?

James says we should pray for each other for good reason. Praying to God on the behalf of others demonstrates a willingness to place the needs of others above our own interests, and it shows a selflessness that's directly tied with submission to God. It's also a way of practicing what James taught earlier: "love your neighbor as yourself" (James 2:8).

James also tells us to confess our sins to one another. By confessing our sins to other believers, we can be held accountable for our words and actions, receive help when we need it, and gain the support we need to correct our own bad behavior. Also, exposing our flaws and failures to each other is an act of humility, and having a heart of humility is also directly tied with submission (James 4:6–7).

❁ DIGGING DEEPER

READ JAMES 5:19–20.

7. What does James say can happen to a person in this verse?

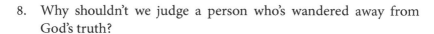

REREAD JAMES 4:11–12.

8. Why shouldn't we judge a person who's wandered away from God's truth?

READ ROMANS 13:8.

9. By judging someone who's wandered away from God, what are we failing to demonstrate?

READ GALATIANS 6:1–2.

10. If we shouldn't judge someone struggling with sin, what should we do instead?

11. How is trying to bring a person back to God an act of selflessness?

Both James and Paul tell us we're to pay attention and notice when anyone is in danger of wandering away from God. They also tell us that it's our job to help bring that person back. By noticing and acting when someone has wandered away from God's truths, we demonstrate that we genuinely care about others, and the command from God to love unconditionally becomes evident. Instead of judging, condemning, and destroying others, we should behave selflessly by *gently* leading those who stray back into a right relationship with God. That's the opposite of judging—that's selflessness, love, and grace.

REREAD JAMES 4:12.

12. Who does James say can save and destroy through judgment?

READ GALATIANS 5:14–15.

13. If we as humans turn on others in judgment, what will we end up doing?

REREAD JAMES 5:20.

14. How does James say we can save a person?

15. What happens when we turn someone away from their sin?

James makes it clear that only God's judgment can result in salvation. When *we* judge each other, on the other hand, all we can do is condemn each other. None of us has the power to save people from spiritual death—that power belongs to God and God alone. So when we see someone sinning or turning away from God, judgment is absolutely the wrong response, because we can only cause more problems. Instead, we should reach out to others with love. It's only by *not* judging others that we have any chance of bringing a person back to God and restoring their rights as believers. If we show others complete and selfless love, they can be brought to God and *he* can do the saving.

❁ SOMETHING TO THINK ABOUT: THE POWER OF SUBMISSION

James has been telling us *how* to submit to God, *why* we should submit to God, and what submission to God *looks like*. In this chapter he takes the topic of submission to its powerful conclusion: through submission, we can help others *attain salvation*.

James explains that we have incredible power at our disposal when we choose to submit to God. This power transforms and purifies our hearts; it gives us new life and victory over a corrupt world. This power reveals godly wisdom, strengthens faith, produces righteousness, and lets our good deeds create lasting impressions. This power can even lead people back to God

Look at the power of the apostles. They turned the whole world upside down with their message of salvation because they believed, submitted to God's desires, and *acted* as he would have them act. The same with Paul. He was educated, powerful, and respected by the community. But he walked away from that affirmation, submitted to God, and committed himself to God's mission. In turn, he founded many churches, led countless others to salvation in Christ, and authored much of the New Testament. All this was possible because Paul and the apostles took submission seriously and devoted themselves to living it.

We have that same power available to us, if only we are willing to shed the things that give us earthly satisfaction. If we are willing to submit to God, if we are willing to focus on serving and loving others, then this power is ours. Belief is not enough; "even the demons believe" (James 2:19). Instead we must act on that belief, bringing faith and works together. And by submitting to God our faith grows stronger, our good works come naturally, and the power of God that works through us will be seen by everyone. Along the way, we will even bring others to Christ. That is true, lasting power!

Conclusion

Many believers consider the book of James to be a how-to guide on being a follower of God, and after studying it in its entirety, we can clearly see why. But while it's true that the letter is filled with practical advice on how to live Christian lives, James delivers so much more to his readers.

The book of James is really all about our relationship with God. James forces us to take a closer look at that relationship and realize that the only way to live a good Christian life is by getting right with God. That means putting aside our own selfish needs and desires; it means living for God and for other people.

Paul agrees with James about this. Paul's teachings on faith, obedience, and love coincide and complement what James teaches in his letter. By considering what both men have to say on these subjects, we are better able to critically examine our own beliefs, behaviors, and attitudes.

But for James, the bottom line is submission. First and foremost, we must submit our lives to God. It's only through submission that we'll receive the power to display correct godly behavior, help people around us, and lead others to God. If we let it, this power will change our attitudes, behaviors, and lives, transforming us into the followers that God desires. James says it, and Paul confirms it.

So let's take what we've learned in the book of James and apply it to our own lives. Rather than living for ourselves and for the world, let's instead live for God and see what great and wondrous things he has in store.

Praise be to God forever and ever!

Lightning Source UK Ltd.
Milton Keynes UK
UKOW07f0013281114

242327UK00015B/352/P